YOSEMITE GUIDE BOOK 2023

A Comprehensive Travel Guide
Book 2023 To Experience The Best
of Yosemite National Park In 5-
days With 20 Exceptional Activities
You Must Do On The Yosemite

NICHOLAS INGRAM

WELCOME TO
YOSEMITE NATIONAL PARK

"Amidst nature's grandeur, Yosemite's embrace beckons.

Through towering sequoias and majestic waterfalls,

Discover a sanctuary where wilderness and wonder intertwine.

Let the mountains guide your spirit,

And the beauty of this pristine landscape ignite your soul.

Welcome to Yosemite, where adventure awaits at every turn."

COPYRIGHT

ABOUT THE AUTHOR

Nicholas Ingram is a travel writer and photographer who has visited over 50 countries. He is the author of several travel guides, under the "The World Explorer" travel guide series on Amazon which includes travel guides to Athens, Lisbon, Morocco, Malta, Amsterdam, Costa-Rica And Many other places.

Nick is passionate about helping people discover new places and experiences. He believes that travel is the best way to learn about different cultures and broaden one's horizons.

In his spare time, Nick enjoys hiking, biking, and spending time with his family.

ABOUT THIS GUIDE

Welcome to the "YOSEMITE GUIDE BOOK 2023: A Comprehensive Travel Guide Book to Explore and Enjoy 17 Exceptional and Unique Natural Wonders at Yosemite National Park in 5 Days." This guide is your ultimate companion to discovering the breathtaking beauty of Yosemite National Park, one of nature's greatest masterpieces.

Packed with comprehensive information, insider tips, and detailed itineraries, this guide is designed to help you make the most of your visit to Yosemite. Whether you're an adventure enthusiast, a nature lover, or simply seeking tranquility in the midst of awe-inspiring landscapes, this guidebook has you covered.

Inside, you'll find a wealth of essential information on the park's iconic landmarks, hidden gems, and lesser-known trails. Explore towering granite cliffs, majestic waterfalls, ancient sequoia groves, and pristine meadows as you navigate through the pages. Detailed maps, trail descriptions, and suggested activities will ensure that you don't miss a single highlight.

Our carefully curated itineraries cater to different interests and time constraints, allowing you to tailor your experience to suit your preferences. Whether you have five days to immerse yourself in the park's wonders or are looking for shorter excursions, you'll find options that suit your needs.

In addition to providing practical guidance, this guidebook emphasizes the importance of responsible travel. Learn about Leave No Trace principles, wildlife conservation, and how to minimize your impact on the environment. By following these guidelines, we can all contribute to preserving Yosemite's natural splendor for future generations.

Please note that while every effort has been made to ensure accuracy, the dynamic nature of the park may lead to changes in trail conditions, access, or visitor facilities. We recommend consulting official park sources or visitor centers for the most up-to-date information during your trip.

Embark on an unforgettable journey through Yosemite National Park with the "YOSEMITE GUIDE BOOK 2023." Let the wonders of nature captivate you as you create memories that will last a lifetime. Enjoy your adventure!

What Is Included In This Travel Guide?

This extensive travel manual serves as a valuable tool to assist you in organizing your excursion to Yosemite National Park. It encompasses a wide range of details, including the best time to visit, where to stay, what to do, accommodations, attractions, transportation, and essential items to bring. Whether your visit spans a weekend or an entire week, this guide will ensure that you optimize your experience in Yosemite.

How To Use This Travel Guide

This travel guide is designed to be used in a variety of ways. You can use it to plan your trip from start to finish, or you can use it as a reference guide while you're in Yosemite.

If you're planning your trip, start by reading the chapters on the history, significance, and best time to visit. This will give you a good understanding of the park and its offerings.

Once you know when you're going, you can start planning your itinerary. The chapters on camping, accommodation, food, and activities will give you ideas for things to do.

If you're traveling with children, be sure to read the chapter on family-friendly activities. This chapter includes a variety of activities that are perfect for families of all ages.

No matter how you use this travel guide, we hope you find it helpful. Yosemite is a beautiful and awe-inspiring place, and we want you to have the best possible experience.

CONTENTS

INTRODUCTION

ABOUT THE YOSEMITE NATIONAL PARK

Yosemite National Park, situated amidst the majestic Sierra Nevada Mountains in California, is an extraordinary realm of unrivaled splendor and remarkable natural phenomena. Within its boundaries, awe-inspiring panoramas, majestic granite cliffs, cascading waterfalls, and untouched wilderness harmoniously blend together, forming an indelible encounter that will be etched in your memory forever.

Encompassing a vast expanse of more than 750,000 acres, Yosemite is celebrated for its varied ecosystems and distinctive geological characteristics. This renowned national park holds a cherished spot in the hearts of nature enthusiasts, adventurers, and individuals in search of solace amidst the grandeur of the natural world.

Yosemite's history dates back thousands of years, with evidence of human habitation by Native American tribes such as the Ahwahneechee people. The park's name, "Yosemite," is derived from the native word "Yohhe'meti," meaning "some among them are killers," a reference to the renowned and awe-inspiring waterfalls that grace the park's landscape.

In 1864, Yosemite became the first land set aside by the U.S. government for preservation and protection, paving the way for the establishment of the national park system. Today, it stands as a testament to the importance of preserving our natural heritage for future generations.

One of the most iconic features of Yosemite is its remarkable granite cliffs, including the legendary El Capitan and Half Dome. These towering monoliths captivate visitors with their sheer size and majestic presence, inspiring awe and admiration. Witnessing a sunset paint these granite giants in hues of gold and pink is an experience that words cannot fully capture.

Waterfalls are another highlight of Yosemite's landscape,

with Yosemite Falls, Bridalveil Fall, and Vernal Fall among the most renowned. The thundering rush of water cascading down the rugged cliffs is a symphony for the senses, evoking a sense of wonder and reminding us of nature's raw power.

Yosemite's valleys, such as Yosemite Valley and Hetch Hetchy, offer idyllic meadows, serene rivers, and lush forests. The meandering trails that wind through these valleys beckon hikers, inviting them to explore the enchanting wilderness and discover hidden treasures along the way.

For those seeking adventure, Yosemite is a playground of outdoor activities. From hiking and rock climbing to biking, horseback riding, and winter sports, there is something for every adrenaline seeker and nature lover. The park's extensive trail system caters to all skill levels, allowing visitors to immerse themselves in the serenity of the wilderness or challenge themselves on more strenuous paths.

Yosemite's biodiversity is equally astounding, with an array of plant and animal species calling the park home. From majestic black bears and elusive mountain lions to the delicate wildflowers that blanket the meadows, the park's wildlife offers glimpses into the intricate web of life that thrives in this protected sanctuary.

As you embark on your Yosemite adventure, it is important to remember that this park is not only a place of beauty but also a place of preservation. Respecting the park's guidelines and practicing "Leave No Trace" principles ensure that future generations can continue to experience the magic of Yosemite.

In the following chapters of this guidebook, we will delve deeper into Yosemite's wonders, providing you with practical information, insider tips, and a wealth of knowledge to make your visit to Yosemite National Park truly unforgettable. So, lace up your hiking boots, breathe in the fresh mountain air, and prepare to be mesmerized by the awe-inspiring beauty of Yosemite National Park.

BEST TIME TO VISIT

Choosing the right time to visit Yosemite National Park can greatly enhance your experience and allow you to make the most of the park's natural wonders. We'll explore the different seasons and provide insights into the best time to visit Yosemite based on weather, activities, crowds, and natural phenomena.

Spring: Blooming Landscapes And Rushing Waterfalls

Spring in Yosemite brings a burst of new life as wildflowers bloom and waterfalls reach their peak flow. Discover the vibrant colors of the park's flora, including dogwoods, lupines, and poppies, as you explore the verdant meadows and hiking trails. However, be prepared for unpredictable weather and potentially crowded conditions, especially during the popular spring break period.

Summer: Long Days And Outdoor Adventures

Summer is the peak tourist season in Yosemite, offering long daylight hours and a wide range of outdoor activities. Enjoy hiking, rock climbing, and backpacking in the park's high country, and take advantage of clear skies for stargazing. While the weather is generally pleasant, be prepared for larger crowds and the need to make reservations well in advance for accommodations and camping.

Fall: Spectacular Colors And Quieter Trails

Fall is a magnificent time to visit Yosemite, with the park's foliage transforming into vibrant shades of red, orange, and gold. The autumn colors provide a stunning backdrop for photography and hiking adventures. As crowds start to thin, you'll have the opportunity to explore the park's trails and iconic landmarks with more tranquility. However, be aware of potential weather changes and the need for layered clothing.

Winter: Serenity And Snow-Covered Landscapes

Winter in Yosemite offers a peaceful and serene atmosphere, with snow-capped peaks and glistening landscapes. This is an ideal time for cross-country skiing, snowshoeing, and enjoying the park's tranquility. The famous Horsetail Fall Firefall phenomenon also occurs during this time, where the setting sun creates an illusion of a flowing waterfall of fire. However, note that some areas and facilities may be closed or have limited access due to snowfall, and tire chains may be required.

Shoulder Seasons: Spring And Fall Transitions

The intermediary seasons of late spring and early fall provide an ideal equilibrium, combining pleasant weather conditions with reduced crowds. During these transitional periods, you have the chance to relish the finest aspects of both worlds: the vibrant wildflowers and cascading waterfalls of spring, or the breathtaking autumn foliage and serene trails of fall. These seasons present a wonderful opportunity to savor the park's offerings with milder climate and fewer fellow visitors.

It's important to note that the best time to visit Yosemite depends on your personal preferences, desired activities, and tolerance for crowds. Each season has its own unique charm and highlights. By understanding the characteristics of each season, you can plan your visit to Yosemite National Park accordingly, ensuring a memorable and fulfilling experience in this natural wonderland.

ΔΔΔ

WHAT TO PACK

When preparing for a vacation at Yosemite National Park, it's crucial to pack wisely to ensure you have a comfortable and enjoyable experience amidst the park's diverse landscapes and ever-changing weather conditions. Here is a comprehensive list of essential items to consider including in your packing.

Clothing

Layered clothing

Yosemite's weather can vary significantly, so pack a variety of clothing layers to adapt to temperature changes throughout the day.

Waterproof and breathable outer shell

Bring a waterproof jacket or raincoat to stay dry during unexpected showers.

Sturdy hiking boots

Comfortable, broken-in hiking boots with good traction are essential for exploring the park's trails.

Moisture-wicking socks

Pack several pairs of socks that keep your feet dry and prevent blisters.

Hat and sunglasses:

Shield yourself from the sun's rays with a wide-brimmed hat and UV-blocking sunglasses.

Swimsuit and quick-drying towel

If you plan to swim in lakes or rivers, don't forget your swimwear and a fast-drying towel.

Gear And Equipment

Daypack or backpack

A lightweight and spacious daypack is essential for carrying water, snacks, and other essentials during your outings.

Water bottles

Stay hydrated by carrying reusable water bottles and consider a water filter or purification system for refilling along the way.

Trail map and compass

Familiarize yourself with the park's trails and carry a map and compass or a reliable navigation app.

Binoculars

Enhance your wildlife spotting and scenic views by packing a pair of binoculars.

Camera and extra batteries

Capture the stunning landscapes and wildlife encounters, and remember to bring spare batteries or a portable charger.

Portable phone charger

Ensure you can stay connected and have a backup power source for your electronic devices.

Camping gear (if applicable)

If you plan to camp, bring a tent, sleeping bag, sleeping pad, and cooking equipment.

Personal Supplies

Sunscreen and insect repellent

Ensure your skin is protected against the damaging rays of the sun and effectively prevent irritating bug bites by utilizing suitable sunscreen and insect repellent.

Personal hygiene products

Pack travel-sized toiletries, including soap, toothpaste, and a toothbrush.

Medications and first aid kit

Carry any necessary medications and a basic first aid kit for minor injuries or ailments.

Personal identification and park permits

Have your identification documents readily accessible, and obtain any required permits for camping or hiking in advance.

Food And Snacks

High-energy snacks

Include lightweight, non-perishable snacks like trail mix, energy bars, and dried fruits in your pack to sustain your energy levels during hikes.

Meals and cooking supplies (if camping)

If you plan to cook your meals, bring lightweight, easy-to-prepare food items and the necessary cooking utensils.

Remember to pack responsibly and adhere to Leave No Trace principles by minimizing waste and respecting the natural environment. By being well-prepared, you'll be able to fully enjoy your vacation at Yosemite National Park and make lasting memories amidst its breathtaking beauty.

△△△

HOW TO GET TO YOSEMITE

Yosemite National Park can be accessed through various transportation options.

By Plane

If you prefer to travel by air, the nearest major airport is Fresno Yosemite International Airport (FAT), located approximately 65 miles from the park. Additionally, there are smaller airports in the vicinity, such as Merced Regional Airport (MCE) and Mammoth Yosemite Airport (MMH).

Upon landing at any of these airports, you have the choice of renting a car or utilizing shuttle services to reach Yosemite National Park.

By Train

Amtrak provides train transportation to Merced, located approximately 45 miles away from Yosemite National Park. From Merced, it is possible to either hire a car or utilize a shuttle service to reach the park.

By bus

YARTS (Yosemite Area Regional Transportation System) provides bus transportation to Yosemite National Park from various cities in the vicinity, such as Fresno, Merced, Mariposa, and Oakhurst.

By Car

Yosemite National Park is situated in the Sierra Nevada mountains, approximately 250 miles to the east of San Francisco and 300 miles to the south of Sacramento. To reach the park by car, you can take Highway 120, Highway 140, or Highway 41.

By Boat

There are no boat services available to reach Yosemite National Park. Regardless of the transportation method you select, it is crucial to plan ahead and allocate ample time for your journey. Yosemite National Park is a highly popular destination, and traffic can be substantial, particularly during the peak season, which is usually in the summer.

WHERE TO STAY

There are several options for where to stay in Yosemite National Park.

Inside The Park

There are three lodging options inside Yosemite National Park:

The Ahwahnee Hotel

This historic hotel is located in Yosemite Valley and offers stunning views of the park's waterfalls and granite cliffs.

Yosemite Valley Lodge

This lodge is also located in Yosemite Valley and offers a variety of amenities, including a restaurant, bar, and gift shop.

Wawona Hotel

This historic hotel is located in the southern part of the park and is near the Mariposa Grove of Giant Sequoias.

Outside The Park

There are also several lodging options outside Yosemite National Park. These options include hotels, motels, bed and breakfasts, and vacation rentals.

Camping

Yosemite National Park features multiple campgrounds that provide a range of amenities for visitors. These amenities include facilities such as restrooms, showers, and fire rings, enhancing the camping experience for guests.

Whichever option you choose, be sure to book your accommodations in advance, especially during the peak season (summer).

Here are some additional tips for choosing where to stay in Yosemite National Park:

Consider your budget

Accommodation options in Yosemite National Park range in price from budget-friendly campgrounds to luxurious hotels.

Think about your interests

If you're looking for a place to relax and enjoy the scenery, you might want to stay in Yosemite Valley. If you're looking for more activities and amenities, you might want to stay in one of the gateway communities outside the park.

Book your accommodations in advance

Yosemite National Park is a popular destination, and accommodations can fill up quickly, especially during the peak season (summer).

WHERE TO EAT

There are several places to eat in Yosemite National Park, including:

Inside The Park

The Ahwahnee Dining Room

This fine-dining restaurant offers stunning views of Yosemite Valley and a seasonal menu of American cuisine.

The Majestic Yosemite Hotel

This historic hotel offers a variety of dining options,

including a casual restaurant, a bar, and a coffee shop.

Yosemite Valley Lodge

This lodge offers a variety of dining options, including a casual restaurant, a bar, and a coffee shop.

Curry Village

This village offers a variety of dining options, including a pizza place, a deli, and a grill.

Wawona Hotel

This historic hotel offers a variety of dining options, including a casual restaurant, a bar, and a coffee shop. Outside the park

There are also several dining options in the gateway communities outside Yosemite National Park, including restaurants, cafes, and fast food chains.

Campgrounds

There are also several campgrounds in Yosemite National Park that offer food service, including Tuolumne Meadows

Campground, Glacier Point Campground, and Wawona Campground.

Regardless of the choice you make, it is important to make advance reservations, particularly during the peak season (summer). Ensuring your reservations are secured ahead of time will help to avoid any potential inconveniences and ensure a smooth experience.

GETTING AROUND YOSEMITE

There are several ways to get around Yosemite National
Park.

BY CAR

Yosemite National Park is a large park, and the best way to
see it is by car. There are several scenic drives in the park,
including Tioga Road, Glacier Point Road, and Wawona
Road.

BY BUS

YARTS (Yosemite Area Regional Transportation System) provides bus transportation to Yosemite National Park from various cities in the surrounding area, including Fresno, Merced, Mariposa, and Oakhurst.

BY BIKE

There are several bike trails in Yosemite National Park, including the Yosemite Valley Bicycle Path and the Glacier Point Road Bicycle Path.

BY FOOT

Yosemite National Park offers an excellent hiking experience with a variety of trails suited for different levels of difficulty.

BY SHUTTLE

The Yosemite Valley Shuttle is a free shuttle that runs throughout Yosemite Valley. The shuttle is a great way to get around the valley without having to worry about parking.

BY HORSEBACK

There are several companies that offer horseback riding tours in Yosemite National Park.

BY MULE

There are several companies that offer mule rides to Glacier Point in Yosemite National Park.

BY BOAT

Various enterprises provide boat excursions within Yosemite National Park, encompassing the Merced River and Curry Village Boat Docks.

ACCOMODATION

When it comes to budget-friendly accommodations in Yosemite National Park, there are a few options you can consider. Keep in mind that prices may vary depending on the season and availability, so it's advisable to check the latest rates before making any reservations. Here are some budget-friendly hotels in and around Yosemite National Park:

7 BUDGET-FRIENDLY HOTELS AT THE YOSEMITE

Yosemite Valley Lodge

This lodge offers reasonably priced rooms and is located in the heart of Yosemite Valley. It provides easy access to popular attractions like Yosemite Falls and Half Dome. The lodge features comfortable rooms, a food court, a bar, and other amenities.

Curry Village

Village offers a range of affordable accommodations,

including canvas tents and rustic cabins. It's a popular option for budget travelers and is conveniently located close to the base of Glacier Point and the trailheads to Nevada and Vernal Falls.Tent cabins are the most budget-friendly option, starting at $100 per night.

Cedar Lodge

Situated just outside the western entrance of Yosemite National Park, Cedar Lodge provides affordable rooms and amenities like an outdoor pool and a hot tub. It's a good option for those who want to explore the park's western side.

Yosemite Westgate Lodge

Located near the park's Big Oak Flat entrance, Yosemite Westgate Lodge offers budget-friendly rooms with basic amenities. It provides easy access to attractions like Hetch Hetchy Reservoir and Tuolumne Meadows.

Yosemite International Hostel: If you're open to a hostel experience, the Yosemite International Hostel in Groveland is an affordable option. It offers dormitory-style rooms, private rooms, and communal spaces where travelers can interact with each other.

Wawona Hotel

This historic hotel offers a variety of lodging options, including standard rooms, cabins, and cottages. Standard rooms are the most budget-friendly option, starting at $150 per night.

Yosemite Bug Rustic Mountain Resort

This resort offers a variety of lodging options, including tent cabins, canvas cabins, and standard rooms. Tent cabins are the most budget-friendly option, starting at $100 per night.

The Big Trees Lodge

This lodge offers a variety of lodging options, including standard rooms, cabins, and cottages. Standard rooms are the most budget-friendly option, starting at $150 per night.

Remember to check the amenities, availability, and cancellation policies of each hotel before making your reservation. Additionally, if you're planning to visit during peak season, it's advisable to book well in advance to secure the best rates.

4 MID-RANGE HOTELS AT THE YOSEMITE

Mid-range hotels in Yosemite National Park offer comfortable accommodations at a reasonable price. These hotels provide a pleasant stay for visitors without breaking the bank. Here are some mid-range hotels to consider:

Yosemite Valley Lodge

Yosemite Valley Lodge is located in Yosemite Valley, just steps from Yosemite Falls. The lodge offers a variety of lodging options, including standard rooms, cabins, and cottages. Standard rooms start at $200 per night.

The Redwoods In Yosemite

The Redwoods In Yosemite is located in Fish Camp, just outside of Yosemite Valley. The hotel offers a variety of lodging options, including standard rooms, cabins, and cottages. Standard rooms start at $250 per night.

Standard rooms at the **Wawona Hotel** start at $250

per night while Tent cabins at the **Yosemite Bug Rustic Mountain Resort** start at $200 per night.

7 LUXURY HOTELS AT THE YOSEMITE

Yosemite National Park offers a selection of luxurious hotels that provide exceptional accommodations and top-notch amenities. These luxury hotels ensure a lavish and memorable experience for guests. Here are some of the luxury hotels at Yosemite National Park:

The Ahwahnee

The Ahwahnee Hotel can be found in Yosemite Valley, a mere stone's throw away from the majestic Yosemite Falls. The Ahwahnee is recognized as a National Historic Landmark renowned for its grand architecture and elegant ambiance. It offers luxurious rooms and suites with breathtaking views of the park. Guests can indulge in fine dining, spa services, and various recreational activities. The starting price for standard rooms is $500 per night.

Tenaya Lodge At Yosemite

Situated in Fish Camp, California, just outside of Yosemite National Park, Tenaya Lodge at Yosemite is a distinguished

AAA Four Diamond resort. The lodge provides a range of lodging options, including standard rooms, suites, and cabins adorned with upscale furnishings Guests can indulge in numerous amenities offered by Tenaya Lodge, such as a spa, fitness center, swimming pool, a selection of restaurants and outdoor activities such as hiking and horseback riding.

Rush Creek Lodge

Located near the park's entrance, Rush Creek Lodge offers a luxurious wilderness experience. The lodge features upscale rooms and spacious suites with modern amenities. Guests can relax at the spa, savor gourmet cuisine, and unwind by the pool or around the outdoor fire pits.

Château Du Sureau

Situated in Oakhurst, a short drive from Yosemite, Château du Sureau is a charming luxury hotel. It offers luxurious suites and cottages with refined décor and personalized service. Guests can enjoy gourmet dining, a European-style spa, and tranquil gardens.

The Majestic Yosemite Hotel

Yosemite Valley is home to The Majestic Yosemite Hotel, conveniently situated across from the breathtaking

Yosemite Falls. This hotel provides remarkable vistas of the park and serves as an excellent choice for families. Standard rooms can be booked starting at $400 per night.

The Post Ranch Inn

The Post Ranch Inn is located in Big Sur, just outside of Yosemite National Park. The inn offers stunning views of the Pacific Ocean and is a great option for couples. Standard rooms start at $600 per night.

The Auberge Du Soleil

The Auberge du Soleil is located in Rutherford, just outside of Yosemite National Park. The inn offers stunning views of the Napa Valley and is a great option for couples. Standard rooms start at $700 per night.

EATING OUT

Exploring the breathtaking landscapes of Yosemite National Park can work up quite an appetite. Thankfully, the park offers a diverse range of dining options to suit various tastes, ranging from fine dining establishments to laid-back and informal eateries. In this chapter, we will guide you through the culinary delights of Yosemite, highlighting the best places to eat and drink within the park. Here are a few highly recommended restaurants within the park:

6 BUDGET-FRIENDLY RESTAURANTS

If you're looking for budget-friendly dining experiences

in Yosemite National Park, there are several options available to satisfy your hunger without breaking the bank. There are several options available to satisfy your hunger without breaking the bank. Here are some recommended restaurants that offer affordable meals:

The Base Camp Eatery

This informal restaurant offers delicious and affordably priced dishes, such as sandwiches, burgers, salads, and satisfying breakfast choices under $15. It's an excellent spot to recharge and replenish your energy after a day of discovering the park.

Curry Village Pizza Deck

Enjoy delicious and affordable pizza at Curry Village. They offer a variety of toppings and sizes to suit different appetites, making it an ideal spot for a quick and budget-friendly meal. This pizza restaurant offers slices and whole pies for under $15.

Degnan's Kitchen

Located in Yosemite Valley, Degnan's Kitchen serves up affordable comfort food such as burgers, sandwiches, soups, and salads. It's a popular choice for a satisfying meal at reasonable prices. This deli offers a variety of sandwiches, salads, and soups for under $10.

Village Grill At Yosemite Lodge

This casual restaurant offers affordable American-style fare, including burgers, sandwiches, and salads. It's conveniently located near Yosemite Lodge, making it a convenient option for park visitors. This burger joint offers burgers, fries, and shakes for under $15.

Yosemite Valley Food Court

For a range of affordable options in one place, head to the Yosemite Valley Food Court. Here, you'll find various food stations offering diverse cuisines, such as Mexican, Asian, and American, ensuring there's something for everyone's taste and budget.

Yosemite Village Store

This grocery store has a variety of prepared foods, including sandwiches, salads, and pizzas, for under $10.

Remember, these budget-friendly restaurants offer delicious meals without compromising on taste, allowing you to enjoy your dining experience while staying within your budget at Yosemite National Park.

7 MID-RANGE RESTAURANTS

If you're looking for dining options that offer a balance between affordability and a higher quality experience, Yosemite National Park has a range of mid-range restaurants to choose from. Here are some recommended options:

The Ahwahnee Dining Room

This fine dining restaurant offers stunning views of Yosemite Valley and a menu of classic American dishes.

The Majestic Yosemite Hotel Restaurant

This hotel restaurant offers a more casual dining experience with a menu of American favorites.

The Wawona Hotel Dining Room

This hotel restaurant offers a variety of dining options, including a full breakfast buffet, a lunch counter, and a fine dining restaurant.

The Yosemite Valley Lodge Restaurant

This lodge restaurant offers a variety of dining options, including a full breakfast buffet, a lunch counter, and a pizza restaurant.

The Curry Village Food Court

This food court offers a variety of options, including pizza, burgers, and pasta, for under $20.

The Mountain Room Restaurant

Situated in Yosemite Valley, The Mountain Room Restaurant offers a comfortable and inviting atmosphere with views of the park. Their menu features a mix of American and international dishes made with locally sourced ingredients, providing a delightful dining experience.

Big Trees Lodge Dining Room

Nestled within the Big Trees Lodge, this restaurant offers a warm and cozy ambiance. Their menu features hearty, home-style dishes like roasted chicken, grilled salmon, and delectable desserts.

FINE DINING

The Ahwahnee Dining Room

This National Historic Landmark restaurant offers stunning views of Yosemite Valley and a menu of classic American dishes. Some of the dishes that you can try at the Ahwahnee Dining Room include Roasted rack of lamb with mint jelly, grilled salmon with lemon butter sauce, and filet mignon with béarnaise sauce.

The Majestic Yosemite Hotel Dining Room

This hotel restaurant offers a more casual dining experience with a menu of American favorites. Some of the dishes that you can try at the Majestic Yosemite Hotel Dining Room include Chicken pot pie, New York strip steak, and lobster bisque.

The Wawona Hotel Dining Room

This hotel restaurant offers a variety of dining options, including a full breakfast buffet, a lunch counter, and a fine dining restaurant. Some of the dishes that you can try at the Wawona Hotel Dining Room include Roasted chicken with mashed potatoes, grilled pork chops with applesauce, and shrimp scampi.

The Yosemite Valley Lodge Mountain Room

This lodge restaurant offers stunning views of Yosemite Falls and a menu of classic American dishes. Some of the dishes that you can try at the Yosemite Valley Lodge Mountain Room include Prime rib with Yorkshire pudding, salmon with roasted vegetables, and chicken parmesan.

The Curry Village Dining Pavilion

This restaurant offers a variety of dining options, including a full breakfast buffet, a lunch counter, and a pizza restaurant. Some of the dishes that you can try at the Curry Village Dining Pavilion include Pizza, pasta, and burgers.

THINGS TO SEE AND DO

TOP 15 MUST SEE ATTRACTIONS AT THE YOSEMITE NATIONAL PARK

Yosemite National Park is renowned for its natural beauty and iconic landmarks. Here are some of the top attractions that you should not miss when visiting the park:

Waterfalls

Yosemite's waterfalls are among the park's most captivating features, drawing visitors from around the world. From the thunderous roar of Yosemite Falls, the tallest waterfall in North America, to the delicate grace of Bridalveil Fall, each cascade possesses its own unique charm.

Yosemite's waterfalls are formed by melting snow and rainfall, creating captivating displays of beauty and power. Seasonal variations affect their flow, with peak flow occurring in spring and diminished intensity in summer. Optimal viewpoints include Yosemite Falls, Bridalveil Fall, and Glacier Point, offering different perspectives of multiple waterfalls. The Mist Trail hike leads to Vernal Fall and Nevada Fall, providing exhilarating experiences. Waterfall flow is influenced by weather and water availability, making spring the best time to witness their majesty. Prioritize safety by following trails and park regulations. Explore and be amazed by Yosemite's breathtaking waterfalls.

Yosemite Falls

Upper Yosemite Falls as viewed from the trail leading to the top of the falls [Photo by DAVID ILIFF. License: CC BY-SA 3.0]

Yosemite Falls stands as a renowned and awe-inspiring waterfall of immense grandeur. Its three distinct sections —the Upper Falls, Middle Cascades, and Lower Falls— contribute to its overall height of 2,425 feet (739 meters), making it one of North America's tallest waterfalls. During the spring season, when snowmelt surges, Yosemite Falls becomes a captivating spectacle. Visitors are treated to the majestic rush of water, the refreshing mist upon their faces, and a firsthand encounter with nature's captivating beauty in the heart of Yosemite.

Bridalveil Fall

Bridalveil fall Waterfall in Yosemite
National Park, California

Bridalveil Fall, situated in Yosemite National Park, is a graceful and enchanting waterfall that captivates visitors with its delicate beauty. Cascading down a height of 620 feet (189 meters), it creates a veil-like appearance as the water gracefully descends. The fall's name originates from the ethereal mist that swirls around it, resembling a bridal veil. Bridalveil Fall offers a mesmerizing sight year-round, but it becomes particularly breathtaking during the spring when the snowmelt feeds its flow. Visitors can experience the wonder of nature as they witness this elegant waterfall amidst the stunning landscapes of Yosemite.

Vernal Falls

Vernal Falls and Emerald Pool. Looking North from the John Muir Trail coming down from Nevada Falls. The Mist Trail is ascending at the base of the cliff at our feet. [Photo By Richard Wood]

Vernal Fall in Yosemite National Park, California, is a notable waterfall on the Merced River. Standing at 317 feet (96.6 meters), it ranks as the second highest waterfall in Yosemite Valley, trailing behind Yosemite Fall. Vernal Fall is visible both from afar at Glacier Point and up close along the Mist Trail. While its flow decreases by the end of summer, it remains active throughout the year, sometimes dividing into multiple strands instead of a single sheet of water.

Nevada Falls

Nevada Falls (Little Yosemite Valley, Sierra Nevada Mountains, California, USA) [Photo By James St. John]

Nevada Falls is a 609-foot waterfall on the Merced River in Yosemite National Park, California. It is the third highest waterfall in Yosemite Valley, after Yosemite Fall and Vernal Fall. Nevada Falls is located just upstream of Vernal Fall, and can be viewed from the Mist Trail. The waterfall is most impressive in the spring and early summer, when the snowmelt from the Sierra Nevada Mountains is at its peak.

Nevada Falls is a popular tourist destination, and can be crowded during peak season. The hike to Nevada Fall is strenuous, with an elevation gain of 1,600 feet. However, the views from the top of the waterfall are well worth the effort.

Valleys

Yosemite National Park is home to several magnificent valleys that showcase its natural beauty. Here are some notable valleys within the park:
Yosemite Valley

The heart of the park, Yosemite Valley is a must-visit destination. Surrounded by towering granite cliffs and breathtaking waterfalls, it offers stunning views of iconic landmarks such as El Capitan, Half Dome, and Bridalveil Fall.

Hetch Hetchy Valley

This lesser-known but equally beautiful valley offers hiking trails and scenic vistas. The Hetch Hetchy Reservoir, framed by granite cliffs, provides a peaceful setting for exploring nature.

Tuolumne Meadows

A wide spot in the Tuolumne River as it passes through
Tuolumne Meadows [Photo By Moppet65535]

Located at an elevation of 8,600 feet (2,600 meters),
Tuolumne Meadows is a picturesque expanse of alpine
meadows, pristine rivers, and granite domes. It's a fantastic
area for hiking, picnicking, and enjoying the serene beauty
of nature.

Tenaya Canyon

Tenaya Canyon | Photo By David | Flickr

Tenaya Canyon is a deep and rugged valley located between Half Dome and North Dome. It features the spectacular Tenaya Creek and offers opportunities for adventurous hiking and exploration.

Glacier Point

Glacier Point Road, Yosemite National Park, US

Located at an elevation of 7,214 feet (2,199 meters), Glacier Point provides panoramic vistas of Yosemite Valley, including views of Half Dome, Yosemite Falls, and the High Sierra. It's a popular spot for sunrise and sunset photography.

Mariposa Grove

Sequoia Trees in Mariposa Grove [Photo
By Brandon Levinger]

Explore Mariposa Grove to witness the grandeur of giant sequoias, some of the largest and oldest trees on Earth. Take a stroll through this ancient forest and encounter the impressive Grizzly Giant and the California Tunnel Tree.

El Capitan

El Capitan in Yosemite National Park viewed from the Valley Floor | Photo By Mike Murphy

El Capitan, situated in Yosemite Valley, California, is an immense granite monolith. Standing at a staggering height of 3,000 feet above the valley floor, it holds the distinction of being the largest standalone rock formation globally. This awe-inspiring landmark attracts rock climbers from around the world, serving as a coveted destination for their daring expeditions. El Capitan has witnessed numerous legendary climbs, earning its reputation as a site for some of the most demanding and iconic ascents ever accomplished.

Half Dome

Drone Shot of Half Dome in California during Sunset | Photo By Madhu Shesharam

One of the most iconic rock formations in the world, Half Dome captivates visitors with its sheer granite face. Although scaling its summit requires a permit and advanced planning, gazing at its majestic presence is a sight to behold.

Tioga Road

Lone Car On Tioga Road At Olmstead Point
Parking Lot [Photo By David P. Fulmer]

Take a scenic drive along Tioga Road, a highway that winds through the park's high country. Enjoy breathtaking vistas, alpine lakes, and opportunities for hiking, photography, and wildlife viewing.

Yosemite Valley View

Yosemite Valley View Sunset View | Photo
By Christopher Chan | Flickr

Located along Northside Drive, Yosemite Valley View offers
a classic vista of Yosemite Valley, including El Capitan and
Bridalveil Fall. It's an excellent spot for capturing postcard-
worthy photographs.

Mist Trail

Mist Trail | Photo By Masa | Flickr

Embark on the Mist Trail, a popular hiking trail that leads to Vernal Fall and Nevada Fall. Prepare to be drenched in refreshing mist as you ascend the granite steps and enjoy the stunning views along the way.

CULTURAL HERITAGE AT THE YOSEMITE NATIONAL PARK

Yosemite National Park is a beautiful and awe-inspiring place, but it is also a place with a rich history and culture. There are many opportunities to experience the park's cultural heritage, from visiting museums and galleries to attending events and festivals.

The Yosemite Museum

Situated in Yosemite Village, the Yosemite Museum houses displays that delve into the history, geology, and natural wonders of the park.

Ranger-Led Program

Ranger-led programs are a great way to learn about the park's natural and cultural history. Programs are offered on a variety of topics, including hiking, wildlife, and geology.

The Ansel Adams Gallery

The Ansel Adams Gallery is located in Yosemite Village and has exhibits on the life and work of Ansel Adams, one of the most famous photographers of Yosemite National Park.

Cultural Event

There are a variety of cultural events held in Yosemite National Park throughout the year, including music festivals, art shows, and film screenings.

8 OUTDOOR ACTIVITIES YOU
CAN DO ON YOSEMITE

Yosemite National Park offers a haven for hiking enthusiasts, boasting an extensive network of trails that spans over 800 miles. Within the park's boundaries, one can encounter diverse landscapes, ranging from majestic granite cliffs to verdant forests and picturesque high-elevation meadows. Catering to hikers of every skill level, Yosemite presents an array of trails, ranging from leisurely strolls to demanding ascents.

Here are some of the most popular hiking trails in Yosemite National Park:

Trail Hiking

Glacier Point Trail

The Glacier Point Trail provides a chance to witness awe-inspiring panoramas of Yosemite Valley, Half Dome, and Yosemite Falls. Covering a total distance of 4.8 miles round-trip, this trail beckons visitors to fully embrace the captivating beauty of the park. Open for exploration from May to October, the trail offers a moderate level of challenge, catering to passionate hikers in search of a rewarding adventure. To ensure optimal comfort and avoid the intense heat of midday, it is recommended to embark on the hike during the serene hours of early morning or evening.

The Mariposa Grove Trail

The Mariposa Grove Trail is a 2-mile loop trail that winds through the largest grove of giant sequoia trees in Yosemite National Park. The trail is located in the southern part of the park and is open year-round. The trail is moderately easy and is suitable for all ages.

The Yosemite Falls Trail

The Yosemite Falls Trail spans 4 miles round-trip and culminates at the foot of the grand Yosemite Falls, the tallest waterfall in North America. Located within Yosemite Valley and open to visitors from May to October, this trail presents a moderate level of exertion, and it is advisable to embark on the hike during the cooler hours of morning or evening to avoid the heat of the day. Renowned for its spectacular vistas of the falls and the encircling mountains, the trail remains a popular destination and may experience crowding, particularly in the summer season.

The Mirror Lake Trail

The Mirror Lake Trail is a 2-mile round-trip trail that leads to a beautiful lake that reflects the surrounding mountains. The trail is located in Yosemite Valley and is open from May to October. The trail is moderately easy and is suitable for all ages.

The trail begins at shuttle stop #17 and follows Tenaya Creek through a forest of pines and firs. The trail then climbs up to a meadow where Mirror Lake is located. The lake is surrounded by granite cliffs and reflects the surrounding mountains, making it a popular spot for photography.

The trail is a great option for families and hikers of all levels. It is a short and easy hike that offers stunning views of Yosemite Valley.

John Muir Trail

The John Muir Trail (JMT) extends for a remarkable 211 miles as a renowned long-distance hiking trail traversing the magnificent Yosemite National Park. Revered as one of the premier hiking trails in the United States, it treats adventurers to awe-inspiring vistas of majestic mountains, profound canyons, and untouched lakes that exude pristine beauty.

The JMT begins in Yosemite Valley and passes through Tuolumne Meadows, Mount Whitney, and Sequoia National Park. It is a challenging hike that requires a high level of fitness and experience. The trail is often steep and rugged, and it crosses high mountain passes that can be snow-covered well into the summer.

In addition to hiking, there are a variety of other outdoor activities to enjoy in Yosemite National Park. These include:

Rock Climbing

Yosemite National Park holds global acclaim as an unrivaled hub for rock climbing enthusiasts. Its sheer granite cliffs present a diverse array of challenges suitable for climbers at every skill level, spanning from novices to seasoned experts. Within Yosemite, notable climbing destinations such as Half Dome, El Capitan, and Yosemite Falls entice adventurers with their prominence and allure. Engaging in rock climbing within Yosemite's rugged terrain demands perseverance and skill, but the journey proves immensely rewarding as it unveils breathtaking panoramas that showcase the park's unparalleled natural splendor.

Camping

Yosemite National Park stands as a highly sought-after camping destination, ranking among the top choices in the United States. Within the park, a multitude of camping options cater to various preferences, ranging from convenient car camping to immersive backcountry experiences. With over 500 campsites scattered throughout Yosemite Valley, Tuolumne Meadows, and the captivating high country, visitors have abundant choices to embrace. Opting for camping in Yosemite presents an exceptional opportunity to intimately connect with the park's awe-inspiring natural beauty and encounter its diverse wildlife, fostering unforgettable memories in the process.

Fishing

Yosemite National Park offers an excellent opportunity for fishing enthusiasts. With its extensive network of waterways stretching over 500 miles, along with numerous lakes and reservoirs, the park provides ample fishing spots. Visitors can encounter a diverse range of fish species such as trout, bass, and catfish. Engaging in fishing activities within Yosemite presents a wonderful chance to unwind and appreciate the park's stunning natural landscapes.

Here are some tips for fishing in Yosemite National Park:

1. Get a California fishing license.
2. Be aware of the park's fishing regulations.
3. Respect the park's wildlife.
4. Lave no trace.
5. Rafting and Kayaking

Yosemite National Park has several rivers and lakes that are perfect for rafting and kayaking activities. The Merced River is the most popular river for rafting, while Tenaya Lake is the most popular lake for kayaking. Rafting and kayaking in Yosemite are great ways to experience the park's natural beauty and get some exercise.

Horseback riding

For those who love horseback riding, Yosemite National Park is a top-notch choice. The park offers a wide selection of trails designed specifically for this exhilarating activity, ensuring the perfect setting for riders. These trails offer awe-inspiring views of the park's majestic features, including towering mountains, magnificent sequoia trees, and cascading waterfalls. Embarking on a horseback ride in Yosemite not only immerses you in the park's breathtaking beauty but also provides an opportunity to stay active and enjoy physical exercise.

Here are some tips for horseback riding in Yosemite National Park:

1. Book your ride in advance, as they are popular.
2. Wear comfortable shoes and clothing that you can move around in.
3. Bring a hat and sunscreen, as the sun can be strong in Yosemite.
4. Be respectful of the horses and their handlers.

Scenic Drives

Yosemite National Park boasts breathtaking landscapes that are among the most captivating in the world, and there are numerous captivating routes within the park for scenic drives. Tioga Road, Glacier Point Road, and Mariposa Grove Road are among the favored options, providing awe-inspiring vistas of the park's majestic mountains, colossal sequoia trees, and cascading waterfalls. Taking scenic drives in Yosemite offers an exceptional opportunity to immerse oneself in the park's remarkable natural beauty while also enjoying some physical activity.

Below are recommendations for enjoying scenic drives in Yosemite National Park:

1. Before embarking on your drive, it's essential to verify the road conditions, as certain routes might be inaccessible due to weather or ongoing construction.
2. llocate ample time for your journey since you'll undoubtedly want to make frequent stops to appreciate the magnificent vistas.
3. Remember to bring along a camera to capture the breathtaking scenery you'll encounter.
4. Show consideration for fellow drivers and visitors to the park by practicing respectful driving habits.

Cycling And Mountain Biking

Yosemite National Park is a great place to go cycling and mountain biking. There are over 12 miles of paved bike paths available in Yosemite Valley, as well as many miles of unpaved roads and trails. The park has a variety of cycling and mountain biking trails for all levels of experience, from beginner to expert. Cycling and mountain biking in Yosemite are great ways to experience the park's natural beauty and get some exercise.

Here are some guidelines to keep in mind for cycling and mountain biking adventures in Yosemite National Park:

1. Prior to your excursion, it is crucial to verify the conditions of roads and trails, as some may be inaccessible due to weather conditions or ongoing construction.

2. Allocate an adequate amount of time for your ride, as you'll likely want to pause occasionally to appreciate the scenic vistas.

3. Ensure you have essential items such as a helmet, water, and snacks.

4. Demonstrate respect for other visitors to the park as well as the wildlife you may encounter during your ride.

In this chapter, we have merely explored a fraction of the outdoor pursuits that await you at Yosemite National Park. From thrilling whitewater escapades to tranquil horseback rides and serene fishing expeditions, Yosemite presents a plethora of outdoor activities to cater to every adventurer's preference. Whether you crave heart-pounding adrenaline rushes or peaceful interludes in nature, Yosemite has an abundance of offerings to satisfy all.

SHOPPING IN YOSEMITE

There are a few places to shop in Yosemite National Park. The main shopping area is Yosemite Village, which has a variety of stores, including a grocery store, a clothing store, a gift shop, and a bookstore. There are also a few smaller shops located throughout the park, including a general store at Curry Village and a gift shop at the Wawona Hotel.

Here are some of the stores you can find in Yosemite National Park:

Yosemite Village Store

This store has a wide variety of items, including groceries, camping supplies, souvenirs, and clothing.

Curry Village Gift & Grocery

This store has a smaller selection of items than the Yosemite Village Store, but it is located more conveniently for guests of Curry Village.

Wawona Store

This store is located at the Wawona Hotel and has a selection of groceries, souvenirs, and clothing.

Ansel Adams Gallery

This gallery sells Ansel Adams prints and other photography-related items.

Yosemite Museum Gallery

This gallery sells art and photography related to Yosemite National Park.

To ensure the availability of specific items, it is advisable to consult the park's website or contact the store in advance to verify their stock.

NIGHTLIFE IN YOSEMITE

Yosemite National Park offers limited nightlife due to its remote location, resulting in a scarcity of bars or clubs. However, there are a handful of evening activities available for those seeking entertainment options.

Here are some ideas for things to do in Yosemite National Park at night:

Go Stargazing

Yosemite National Park is a great place to go stargazing. The park is located far away from city lights, so you can see the stars clearly.

Take A Walk Around Yosemite Village

Yosemite Village is the main hub of activity in the park.

There are a few shops and restaurants open in the evening, and you can also take a walk around the village and enjoy the scenery.

Attend A Ranger-Led Program

Ranger-led programs are offered in the evening on a variety of topics, including hiking, wildlife, and geology.

Have A Campfire

If you are camping in the park, you can have a campfire in the evening. This is a great way to relax and enjoy the outdoors.

If you are looking for something more lively, you can drive to the nearby town of Mariposa, which has a few bars and restaurants. However, keep in mind that the town is small and there is not much to do in the evening.

20 EXCEPTIONAL ACTIVITIES YOU MUST EXPERIENCE AT THE YOSEMITE NATIONAL PARK

As you venture deeper into the wonders of Yosemite National Park, it's time to uncover some insider tips and discover the hidden gems that make this place truly extraordinary. We'll share 17 unique and exceptional things you should do in Yosemite National Park to enhance your Yosemite experience.

1. VISIT THE MARIPOSA GROVE OF GIANTS SEQUOIAS

The Mariposa Grove is a collection of sequoia trees found within Yosemite National Park. It houses more than 500 giant sequoias, which are the largest trees on the planet. The trees in the Mariposa Grove are renowned for their age and size, with some individuals surpassing 2,000 years in age and towering over 300 feet tall.

A Giant Sequoia in Mariposa Grove [Image Created By Scott Ableman]

The Mariposa Grove attracts numerous tourists and remains open throughout the year, welcoming visitors by both car and foot.

Multiple options are available for exploring the Mariposa Grove, with the most favored being hiking along the numerous trails that weave through the grove. These trails cater to individuals of all skill levels, offering options ranging from leisurely strolls to more demanding treks.

If you are not up for a hike, you can also drive through the grove on the Mariposa Grove Road. The road offers stunning views of the giant sequoias, and there are several pullouts where you can stop to get out and take pictures.

The Mariposa Grove is open year-round, but the best time to visit is during the spring or fall when the weather is mild. The grove is also a popular destination during the winter, when the trees are covered in snow.

The Mariposa Grove is a beautiful and awe-inspiring place. It is a reminder of the power and majesty of nature. The grove is a must-see for anyone visiting Yosemite National Park.

2. GO ROCK CLIMBING AT THE EL CAPITAN

Yosemite is renowned for its world-class rock climbing opportunities, attracting climbers from around the globe. El Capitan, an enormous granite monolith, stands as a globally renowned mecca for rock climbers. It ranks among the most sought-after destinations for climbers worldwide.

Climbing the El-Capitan [Image by Scott Ableman]

Ascending to the summit of El Capitan typically requires around four days and is widely recognized as one of the most formidable rock climbing endeavors in existence.

Nonetheless, less experienced climbers need not be discouraged, as there are also accessible routes catering to their skill levels. Even if you're not an experienced climber, you can still immerse yourself in the climbing culture by watching climbers scale the granite walls of El Capitan or Half Dome. Join a guided climbing tour or visit climbing shops within the park to learn more about this exhilarating sport.

3. TAKE A WALK THROUGH THE ANSEL ADAMS WILDERNESS

The Ansel Adams Wilderness is a vast wilderness area that is home to towering granite peaks, deep canyons, and pristine lakes.

The wilderness is located in the eastern part of Yosemite National Park and is open year-round. There are a variety of hiking trails available in the Ansel Adams Wilderness, ranging from easy walks to challenging hikes.

The Ansel Adams Wilderness is a beautiful and rugged place, and I am sure you would enjoy the scenery and the peace and quietness that comes with walking through it.

Alger Lakes Located on the Ansel Adams Wilderness

You should start your walk at the Agnew Meadows trailhead. This is a popular starting point for many hikes in the wilderness, and it is a great place to get a feel for the landscape. From the trailhead, you should follow the John Muir Trail north. This trail winds through the wilderness, and it offers stunning views of the surrounding mountains and lakes.

You would hike for several hours, enjoying the scenery and the fresh air. As you hiked, you should keep an eye out for wildlife. The Ansel Adams Wilderness is home to a variety of animals, including deer, bears, and birds.

Eventually, you would reach your destination, which is a small lake nestled in the mountains. You should spend some time relaxing by the lake, taking in the beauty of your surroundings. After you've had enough relaxation, You should start your hike back to the trailhead.

The hike back would be just as enjoyable as the hike out. You should take my time, savoring the last few moments of your time in the wilderness. When you finally reached the trailhead, You would have been tired but happy. You will surely have a wonderful day exploring the Ansel Adams Wilderness.

4. GO CAMPING IN TUOLUMNE MEADOWS

Situated in the eastern region of Yosemite National Park, Tuolumne Meadows is a picturesque meadow nestled at high elevation. This idyllic landscape is encircled by majestic granite peaks, creating a breathtaking backdrop.

Tuolumne Meadows At Sunset

Renowned as a favored spot for camping, hiking, and fishing, Tuolumne Meadows allures outdoor enthusiasts from far and wide. It is accessible to visitors from June to September, allowing for a limited but rewarding window to explore its natural splendor.

5. GO HORSEBACK RIDING

Horseback Riding At The Yosemite National Park

Several companies provide horseback riding tours, allowing visitors to explore the park's enchanting beauty from a distinctive vantage point. Engaging in horseback riding offers a wonderful opportunity to witness the park's splendor while immersing yourself in a unique experience. Discovering Yosemite's magnificence from atop a horse provides a fresh perspective and adds a touch of adventure to your journey.

6. GO WHITE-WATER RAFTING, SWIMMING AND FISHING ON THE MERCED RIVER

White-water rafting on the Merced River is a popular activity in Yosemite National Park. The river flows through the park and offers a variety of rapids for all levels of experience. The Merced River is a Class III-IV river, which means that it has some challenging rapids. However, there are also some calmer sections of the river that are perfect for beginners.

Swimming in the Merced River can provide a rejuvenating and pleasant experience amidst the summer months in Yosemite National Park.

Nevertheless, it is crucial to recognize the potential hazards associated with this activity. The river's swift currents and cold temperatures can pose risks and should not be underestimated.

Fishing: The diverse aquatic ecosystem of the Merced River hosts an assortment of fish species, including trout, bass, and catfish. Fishing stands as a favored pastime within the park, attracting enthusiasts of all skill levels. Along the river, numerous locations offer opportunities for anglers to cast their lines and engage in this popular activity.

7. GO BIRDWATCHING

Yosemite National Park harbors more than 250 bird species. The park attracts many bird enthusiasts who engage in the popular pastime of observing birds. Several locations within the park, such as Tuolumne Meadows, Glacier Point, and Mariposa Grove, offer excellent opportunities for bird watching.

8. TAKE A DRIVE ON TIOGA ROAD

 Tioga Road is a scenic mountain road that winds through the high country of Yosemite National Park. The road is open from June to October and offers stunning views of the park's mountains, meadows, and lakes.

9. VISIT THE YOSEMITE VALLEY VISITOR CENTER

Yosemite Valley Visitor Center

If you're looking to enhance your knowledge of the park, the Yosemite Valley Visitor Center is an outstanding choice. Within its walls, visitors have the opportunity to delve into exhibits focused on the park's enthralling his

tory, remarkable geological features, and intriguing wildlife. Moreover, the center provides captivating ranger-led programs and even features a bookstore, expanding the array of educational experiences to be enjoyed.

10. WITNESS SUNRISE AND SUNSET SPECTACLES

Witnessing a sunrise or sunset in Yosemite is an unforgettable experience. Beat the crowds and find a prime spot to watch the sun paint the sky with vibrant hues.

Glacier Point, Tunnel View, and Olmsted Point are just a few locations that offer breathtaking vistas during these magical moments. Capture the beauty with your camera or simply immerse yourself in the serene atmosphere.

11. HIGH SIERRA CAMPS

The High Sierra Camps in Yosemite National Park are a collection of rustic lodges that offer a unique and comfortable way to explore the park's backcountry. Spread about 5 to 10 miles apart, the camps provide manageable daily distances for hikers, with a total trek of approximately 50 to 60 miles over several days.

The trails leading to the camps take you through breathtaking landscapes, including meadows, lakes, and mountain passes, surrounded by majestic peaks and serene forests.
Each camp offers basic amenities like canvas tent cabins, cozy beds, and delicious meals prepared by the staff.

The communal areas allow hikers to relax, socialize, and share their adventure stories.

Disconnecting from the outside world, the High Sierra Camps let you immerse yourself in nature's beauty. Away from technology and modern conveniences, you can appreciate the simplicity and tranquility of the backcountry.

Glen Aulin Tent Cabin, Yosemite National Park

Wildlife encounters are common, including marmots, deer, and possibly black bears. Keep your camera ready to capture these memorable sightings.

The trek through the camps offers ever-changing landscapes and the unique beauty of each season. From blooming wildflowers in spring to golden aspens in fall, you'll witness the magic of Yosemite's high country.

Being physically demanding, it's crucial to be prepared with appropriate gear and navigational tools. Sturdy boots, layered clothing, a reliable backpack, water, snacks, maps, and a compass are essential.

Whether you complete the entire loop or choose a shorter section, the High Sierra Camps trek guarantees unforgettable memories and a deep connection with Yosemite's wilderness. It's a chance to disconnect, reconnect with nature, and discover hidden gems while enjoying the comfort and camaraderie of the camps.

12. GO STARGAZING AT YOSEMITE VALLEY

Yosemite Valley offers a fantastic stargazing experience due to its remote location and dark skies. Away from city lights, the park provides an unparalleled view of the night sky. Under its dark expanse, you'll be captivated by countless stars, distant galaxies, and the Milky Way.

Stargazing in Yosemite Valley allows you to connect with the vastness of the universe and contemplate our place within it. Choose a secluded spot, away from artificial lights, to set up your telescope or simply lay back and marvel at the celestial wonders.

Remember to dress warmly and use a stargazing app or guidebook to identify constellations. This awe-inspiring experience reminds us of the beauty beyond our planet and offers a chance to reconnect with the mysteries of the cosmos.

13. VALLEY FLOOR TOUR

The Valley Floor Tour in Yosemite offers an immersive experience to explore the stunning Yosemite Valley. Hop on a guided tour or rent a bike to discover the park's rich history, fascinating geology, and diverse wildlife. As you journey through the valley floor, knowledgeable guides or informative audio guides provide insights into the park's natural wonders.

The tour guides you through picturesque trails and

showcases famous attractions like El Capitan, Half Dome, and Bridalveil Fall. You'll get a chance to experience the awe-inspiring magnificence of the valley firsthand and gain knowledge about its creation throughout history.

Yosemite Valley Floor Tour at Tunnel View overlooking Yosemite Valley

Along the way, keep an eye out for the park's wildlife, including deer, coyotes, and various bird species. The Valley Floor Tour allows you to appreciate the harmonious balance of nature within Yosemite.

Whether you choose to join a guided tour or embark on a self-guided biking adventure, the Valley Floor Tour offers an educational and awe-inspiring experience, immersing you in the history, geology, and vibrant ecosystem of Yosemite Valley.

14. VISIT THE HISTORIC YOSEMITE VALLEY CHAPEL

The Yosemite Valley Chapel is a beautiful and historic building located in the heart of Yosemite National Park. It was built in 1879 and is one of the oldest buildings in the park. The chapel is a non-denominational church and is open to all visitors.

The chapel is a simple structure with a white exterior and a red roof. It has a small bell tower and a stained glass window. The interior of the chapel is just as simple as the exterior. It has a wooden floor, a wooden ceiling, and wooden pews. There is a pulpit at the front of the chapel and a cross on the wall behind it.

The chapel is a popular spot for weddings and other special events. It is also a popular spot for tourists to visit. The chapel is open to the public from 9:00 am to 5:00 pm daily.

Yosemite Valley Chapel [Image created by Wayne Hsieh]

If you are visiting Yosemite National Park, I encourage you to visit the Yosemite Valley Chapel. It is a beautiful and historic building that is sure to add to your experience of the park.

If you are interested in attending a Sunday service at the Yosemite Valley Chapel, the services are held at 9:15 am and 11:00 am. The services are non-denominational and are open to all visitors.

I hope you have a wonderful time visiting the Yosemite Valley Chapel!

15. TAKE A GUIDED HIKE

Yosemite National Park offers a range of guided hikes led by knowledgeable park rangers and naturalists. These hikes provide an excellent opportunity to explore the park's trails while learning about its natural and cultural history.

Led by experienced guides, you'll venture through diverse ecosystems, including meadows, forests, and alpine regions. Along the way, they'll share captivating stories about the park's geological formations, plant and animal life, and indigenous heritage.

From iconic landmarks like Yosemite Falls to the Mist Trail, these guided hikes deepen your understanding of the park's significance and preservation efforts. They cater to various fitness levels and interests, ensuring everyone can participate.

By joining a guided hike in Yosemite, you'll gain insights, stay safe on the trails, and develop a deeper connection to the park's natural wonders and rich history.

16. HIKE TO YOSEMITE FALLS

To hike to Yosemite Falls, one of the most iconic landmarks in Yosemite National Park, follow these steps:

1. Start at the Yosemite Falls Trailhead, located near Camp 4 in Yosemite Valley.

2. Begin the hike early in the day to avoid crowds and ensure ample daylight.

3. The trail is a 7.2-mile loop, consisting of the Lower Yosemite Fall Trail and the Upper Yosemite Fall Trail.

4. Follow the signs for the Lower Yosemite Fall Trail, which is a relatively easy 1-mile round trip leading to the base of the lower falls.

5. After enjoying the lower falls, return to the trailhead and continue on the Upper Yosemite Fall Trail.
6. The Upper Yosemite Fall Trail is strenuous, climbing about 2,700 feet over 3.5 miles. Take breaks, stay hydrated, and pace yourself.

7. Enjoy the breathtaking views along the way, including the stunning Upper Yosemite Fall.

8. At the top, take a moment to rest, refuel, and soak in the panoramic vistas.

9. Descend using the same trail or continue the loop by taking the Yosemite Valley Loop Trail.

10. Stay on designated trails, follow park regulations, and leave no trace of your visit.

Remember to check trail conditions, carry essential supplies, and be prepared for changes in weather. Enjoy your hike to Yosemite Falls and the natural beauty of Yosemite National Park.

17. DRIVE OR HIKE UP TO GLACIER POINT

To reach Glacier Point in Yosemite National Park, you have two options: driving or hiking. Here's how to get there:

Driving:

1. From Yosemite Valley, take the Wawona Road (Highway 41) south for approximately 16 miles.
2. Look for signs indicating the turnoff to Glacier Point and make a right.
3. Follow Glacier Point Road for about 16 miles until you reach the Glacier Point parking area.
4. Park your vehicle and take a short walk to the viewpoint, where you'll be rewarded with breathtaking panoramic views of Yosemite Valley, Half Dome, and the surrounding mountains.

Hiking

1. Begin at the trailhead located near the Four Mile Trailhead in Yosemite Valley.
2. The trail is approximately 4.8 miles long, with a steep ascent of about 3,200 feet.
3. Take the Four Mile Trail, which offers stunning views along the way, including of Yosemite Falls and El Capitan.
4. After a challenging hike, you'll arrive at Glacier Point, where you can rest and admire the incredible scenery.
5. Consider taking the shuttle bus back to Yosemite Valley or hike back down the same trail.

Remember to check trail conditions, carry plenty of water, and wear appropriate footwear. Glacier Point offers a remarkable viewpoint, providing an unforgettable experience of Yosemite's natural wonders.

18. VISIT THE YOSEMITE MUSEUM IN YOSEMITE VALLEY

A visit to the Yosemite Museum in Yosemite Valley promises an enriching and immersive experience into the park's rich cultural and natural history. Here's what you can expect:

Exhibits

The museum showcases a range of exhibits that delve into the Native American tribes, early settlers, and the natural environment of Yosemite. Learn about the Ahwahneechee people, their traditions, artifacts, and their relationship with the land.

Cultural Insights

Gain a deeper understanding of the indigenous culture and their connection to the Yosemite Valley. The museum highlights the traditions, customs, and stories of the Native American tribes that inhabited the region.

Artwork

Explore a collection of indigenous artwork, including baskets, carvings, and contemporary pieces, showcasing the artistic heritage of the region.

Interpretive Programs

The museum often offers interpretive programs, such as demonstrations, talks, and performances, providing further insight into the cultural and natural history of Yosemite.

Gift Shop

Browse through the museum's gift shop, which offers a selection of books, artworks, and unique souvenirs related to Yosemite's history and Native American culture.

Overall, a visit to the Yosemite Museum offers an opportunity to appreciate the diverse cultural heritage and deepen your connection with the park's natural wonders.

19. TREK THE MIST TRAIL

The Mist Trail is a popular hiking trail in Yosemite National Park that leads to Vernal and Nevada Falls. The trail is 4.8 miles round trip and gains 2,000 feet in elevation. It is a strenuous hike, but the views of the falls are well worth the effort.

To trek the Mist Trail in Yosemite National Park, take the free Yosemite Valley Shuttle to the Happy Isles Trailhead. The trailhead is located near the Happy Isles Nature Center.

1. Start at the trailhead located near Happy Isles

2. The Mist Trail is a popular and strenuous 3-mile (round trip) hike to Vernal Fall, or a 7-mile (round trip) hike to Nevada Fall.

3. Begin with a gradual ascent through a forested area, following the signs for the Mist Trail.

4. As you progress, you'll reach a series of steep, granite staircases offering spectacular views of the rushing Merced River and surrounding cliffs.

5. Prepare to get wet as you approach Vernal Fall, as the mist from the waterfall can drench the trail.

6. Exercise caution on the slippery and wet sections of the trail, and use the provided handrails where available.

7. Take your time to enjoy the awe-inspiring beauty of Vernal Fall and its powerful cascades.

8. If you choose to continue to Nevada Fall, the trail becomes steeper and more challenging.
9. Upon reaching Nevada Fall, take a well-deserved break and admire the breathtaking vistas.

10. Return the same way or complete a loop by descending via the John Muir Trail.

Remember to wear appropriate hiking shoes, carry plenty of water, and be prepared for changing weather conditions. The Mist Trail offers an incredible adventure with close-up views of magnificent waterfalls and stunning natural surroundings in Yosemite National Park.

20. OUTDOOR PHOTOGRAPHY

Outdoor photography in Yosemite National Park presents a remarkable opportunity to capture the breathtaking landscapes, iconic landmarks, and diverse wildlife that make the park a photographer's paradise. Here's what to consider for outdoor photography in Yosemite:

1. Timing And Lighting:

Take advantage of the golden hours, around sunrise and sunset, when the soft light enhances the park's beauty. Experiment with different lighting conditions throughout the day for varied moods and perspectives.

2. Iconic Landmarks

Yosemite offers iconic landmarks such as Half Dome, El Capitan, and Yosemite Falls. Explore different viewpoints and angles to capture their grandeur and incorporate them into your compositions.

3. Scenic Trails And Vistas

Embark on a journey along the park's many trails to uncover hidden treasures and breathtaking views. Feel free to explore uncharted territories and lesser-known spots for distinctive angles and exclusive experiences.

4. Wildlife Photography

Yosemite is home to diverse wildlife, including black bears, deer, and birds. Research their habitats and behavior for the best chances of capturing memorable wildlife shots. Remember to respect their space and keep a safe distance.

5. Weather And Seasons

Yosemite's landscapes transform with the seasons. From the vibrant colors of fall to the snow-capped peaks in winter, each season offers unique photographic opportunities. Plan your visit accordingly and embrace the weather conditions to add depth and character to your images.

6. Composition And Depth

Experiment with composition techniques like leading lines, framing, and foreground elements to create visually captivating images. Utilize the park's diverse elements, such as waterfalls, meadows, and towering cliffs, to add depth and scale to your photographs.

7. Environmental Conservation

While capturing stunning images, prioritize the preservation of Yosemite's natural environment. Follow park regulations, practice leave-no-trace principles, and respect the wildlife and fragile ecosystems.

Outdoor photography in Yosemite is not just about capturing beautiful images but also immersing yourself in the park's awe-inspiring landscapes. Take your time, appreciate the surroundings, and let your creativity flow to create photographs that reflect the essence of this remarkable national park.

6 FAMILY-FRIENDLY ACTIVITIES IN YOSEMITE

Yosemite National Park is a haven for families seeking outdoor adventures and quality time together. In Chapter 12, we will explore the array of family-friendly activities that Yosemite has to offer, ensuring that visitors of all ages can create lasting memories in this remarkable natural wonderland.

JUNIOR RANGER PROGRAM

Immerse your children in the marvels of nature with

Yosemite's Junior Ranger Program. This captivating and enlightening initiative offers kids the opportunity to become esteemed junior rangers by engaging in an array of activities and completing enjoyable workbooks. Through attending ranger-led programs and embarking on nature trails, children will gain knowledge about wildlife, geology, and conservation, all while earning their well-deserved Junior Ranger badge.

EASY HIKES AND NATURE WALKS

Yosemite provides a multitude of easy hikes and nature walks suitable for families with young children. Discover scenic trails like the Lower Yosemite Fall Trail, where you can witness the power and beauty of the waterfall up close. The Bridalveil Fall Trail offers another family-friendly option, leading to an impressive cascade surrounded by stunning natural scenery. These hikes provide an opportunity for children to connect with nature and learn about the park's flora and fauna.

BICYCLE RENTALS AND BIKE PATHS

Explore Yosemite on two wheels by renting bicycles and cycling along the designated bike paths within the park. Enjoy the freedom of pedaling through Yosemite Valley while taking in the breathtaking views of the surrounding mountains and meadows. Bicycles are available for riders of all ages, making it a fun and active way for the whole family to experience the park's beauty.

PICNICKING AND NATURE PLAY AREAS

Take a break from hiking and enjoy a leisurely picnic amidst Yosemite's picturesque landscapes. Numerous designated picnic areas are scattered throughout the park, providing a tranquil setting for a family meal surrounded by nature. Additionally, Yosemite offers nature play areas where children can engage in imaginative play and explore natural features like logs, rocks, and sand, fostering a deeper connection with the outdoors.

RANGER-LED PROGRAMS AND CAMPFIRE TALKS

Join ranger-led programs and campfire talks specially designed for families. These interactive experiences offer opportunities to learn about Yosemite's natural and cultural history through entertaining and educational presentations. From stargazing sessions to wildlife talks, children and adults alike will be captivated by the fascinating stories and knowledge shared by knowledgeable park rangers.

HORSEBACK RIDING

Experience the beauty of Yosemite from a unique perspective by embarking on a family horseback riding adventure. Guided horseback rides are available within the park, allowing families to explore the trails and meadows while enjoying a gentle and scenic journey on horseback. This unforgettable experience will create cherished memories for both children and adults.

Yosemite National Park welcomes families with open arms, providing a wealth of activities that cater to all ages. Whether it's participating in the Junior Ranger Program, embarking on nature walks, or enjoying picnics in serene surroundings, Yosemite offers an ideal setting for families to bond, connect with nature, and create lifelong memories.

T R A V E L
T I P S

TRAVEL TIPS

VISA

Travelers from the majority of countries must acquire a visa to visit the United States.

The application process for a visa entails applying at a US embassy or consulate.

It is recommended to initiate the application early since it can take several weeks to complete.

Along with your passport, you will need to submit a completed visa application form and a recent photograph.

The visa fee differs depending on your nationality.

LANGUAGE

The official language of the United States is English.
However, many people in Yosemite National Park speak other languages, including Spanish, French, and German.

If you do not speak English, it is a good idea to learn some basic phrases before you visit the park.

CURRENCY EXCHANGE

The currency of the United States is the US dollar.
You can exchange your currency at a bank or a currency exchange bureau.

The exchange rate will vary depending on where you exchange your currency.

TIPPING ETIQUETTE

Tipping is customary in the United States.

The amount of the tip is up to you, but it is generally

15-20% of the bill.

You should tip servers, bartenders, hair stylists, and other service providers.

SAFETY AND SECURITY

Yosemite National Park is a safe place to visit.

However, it is important to take some basic safety precautions, such as:

1. Be aware of your surroundings.
2. Do not leave valuables in your car.
3. Do not hike alone in remote areas.
4. Bring plenty of water and food.
5. Be prepared for the weather.
6. Tell someone where you are going and when you expect to be back.

ADDITIONAL TIPS FOR STAYING SAFE IN YOSEMITE

Here are some additional tips for staying safe in Yosemite National Park:

Be Aware Of The Wildlife

Yosemite National Park is home to a variety of wildlife, including bears, deer, and coyotes. Be sure to keep your distance from all wildlife and never feed them.

Be Prepared For The Weather

Yosemite National Park encounters diverse weather conditions, spanning from hot and arid to cold and snowy. It is vital to dress suitably for the prevailing weather and ensure you have an ample supply of water and food.

Stay On The Trails

Yosemite National Park has a network of well-maintained trails. Stay on the trails to avoid getting lost and to protect the park's natural resources.

Leave No Trace

Yosemite National Park is a special place. Be sure to leave no trace of your visit by packing out all of your trash and disposing of it properly.

By following these tips, you can help ensure a safe and enjoyable visit to Yosemite National Park.

5-DAYS FAMILY-FRIENDLY YOSEMITE NATIONAL PARK ITINERARY

DAY 1

Morning

Begin your day with a family-friendly excursion to Lower Yosemite Falls, a leisurely 1-mile round trip hike that is suitable for all ages. Afterward, make your way to the Yosemite Valley Visitor Center, where you can gain a comprehensive understanding of the park and explore the wide array of family-oriented activities it has to offer.

Afternoon

After lunch, take a scenic drive along Tioga Pass Road, stopping at Olmsted Point for breathtaking views of Half Dome and Tenaya Canyon. Continue on to Tuolumne Meadows for a relaxing picnic and some family-friendly activities, such as a game of catch or frisbee.

Evening

Wrap up your day with an unforgettable sunset picnic at Glacier Point, where you can witness the mesmerizing spectacle of the sun gracefully setting over the Yosemite Valley.

Indulge in delectable snacks that are suitable for the whole family while immersing yourselves in the awe-inspiring panorama. Treasure this extraordinary moment as you bask in the splendor of nature unfurling its magnificence before your very eyes.

DAY 2

Morning

Today is all about exploring Yosemite Valley. Start with a

hike to the top of Vernal Falls, a 1.5-mile round trip hike that is suitable for families with older children. After the hike, head to the Ansel Adams Gallery to see some of the famous photographer's stunning black and white images of the park.

Afternoon

After lunch, take a guided tour through the Mariposa Grove of Giant Sequoias, some of the largest trees on Earth. Then, relax by the Merced River and enjoy some family-friendly activities, such as skipping stones or building rock towers.

Evening

End the day with a dinner at the Mountain Room Restaurant, located inside Yosemite Valley Lodge, featuring a kid's menu and locally sourced and sustainable ingredients.

DAY 3

Morning

Today is all about adventure. Start the day with a thrilling whitewater rafting trip down the Merced River. The rafting trip is suitable for families with children over 8 years old. After the adrenaline rush, head to the Yosemite

Mountaineering School to learn how to rock climb or take a guided hike to the top of Lower Yosemite Falls, which is a shorter and easier hike than Vernal Falls.

Afternoon

After lunch, rent a bike and explore the valley on two wheels. Stop at the iconic Ahwahnee Hotel for a mid-afternoon snack and some history about the park's past visitors.

Evening

End the day with a BBQ dinner at Curry Village, where you'll enjoy some of the best ribs and brisket in the area.

DAY 4

Morning

Today's focus is on wildlife. Begin your day with a sunrise wildlife watching tour, providing you with the opportunity to observe black bears, coyotes, and mountain lions in their natural habitat. This tour is suitable for families with children over 6 years old, allowing everyone to partake in this remarkable experience.

Afternoon

After lunch, take a scenic drive to Tioga Pass, stopping at Tenaya Lake for a refreshing swim. Then, continue on to Mono Lake, an otherworldly landscape that's home to millions of migratory birds.

Evening

End the day with dinner at the historic Wawona Hotel, where you'll enjoy classic American cuisine in a charming and rustic setting. The restaurant offers a kid's menu and a family-friendly atmosphere.

DAY 5

Morning

On your final day, embark on a hot air balloon ride over Yosemite Valley for a mesmerizing bird's eye perspective of the park's breathtaking landscapes. This enchanting experience is suitable for families with children over 6 years old, allowing everyone to appreciate the park's stunning scenery from above. Enjoy this unforgettable adventure and create lasting memories together.

Afternoon

After the ride, head to the Yosemite Museum to learn about

the park's Native American history and culture. Then, take a leisurely stroll through Cook's Meadow, a beautiful open space surrounded by towering granite cliffs.

Evening

End the trip with a farewell dinner at the elegant Ahwahnee Dining Room, where you'll enjoy a gourmet meal featuring locally sourced and sustainable ingredients. The restaurant offers a kid's menu and a family-friendly atmosphere.

This suggested 5-day itinerary provides a glimpse into the awe-inspiring marvels of Yosemite National Park, but it's important to note that the park has an abundance of additional attractions. Feel free to customize the itinerary according to your personal preferences and the season you're visiting. Prior to embarking on your adventure, remember to check for any trail closures or restrictions. Embrace the grandeur of nature and craft cherished memories that will endure a lifetime within the remarkable Yosemite National Park.

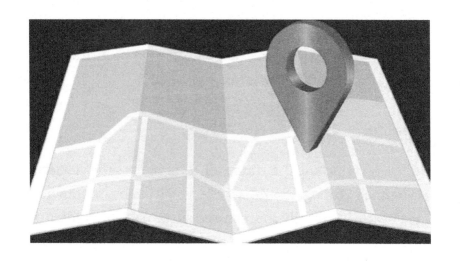

<u>MAPS</u>

It is highly recommended to have a map when visiting Yosemite National Park. Yosemite is a vast and diverse park with numerous trails, landmarks, and points of interest. Having a map will help you navigate the park and locate specific areas you wish to visit, such as popular attractions like Yosemite Valley, Glacier Point, or Tuolumne Meadows.

Added below are some maps you can use to ensure that you don't miss out on any must-see sights or trailheads. They provides valuable information on hiking routes, camping areas, visitor centers, restrooms, and other facilities within the park.

<u>MAP 1</u>

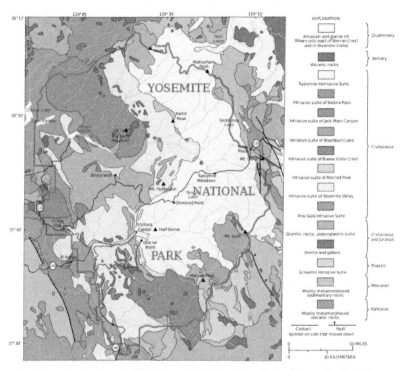

Geological map of Yosemite National Park and vicinity
[Map By The United States Geological Survey]

MAP 2

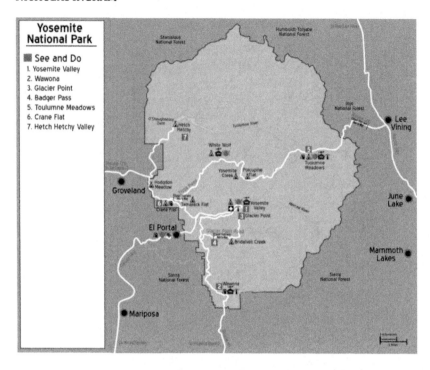

Map of Yosemite National Park showing things
to do [Map created by Nick Roux]

MAP 3

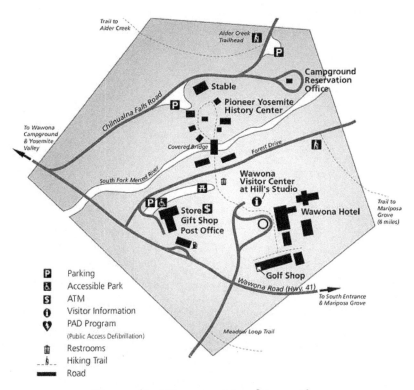

Parking
Accessible Park
ATM
Visitor Information
PAD Program
(Public Access Defibrillation)
Restrooms
Hiking Trail
Road

Yosemite Wawona Map [From the Yosemite park newspaper]

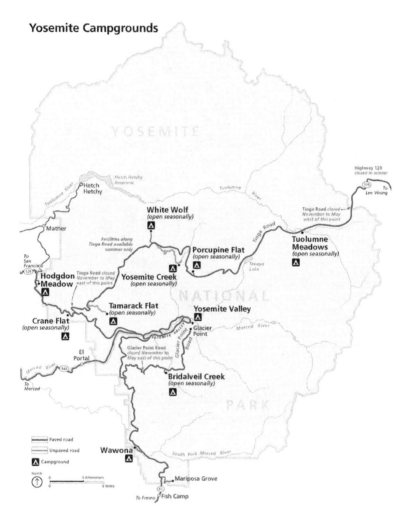

MAP 4: Yosemite Campgrounds [U.S. National Park Service via Picryl.com]

MAP 5

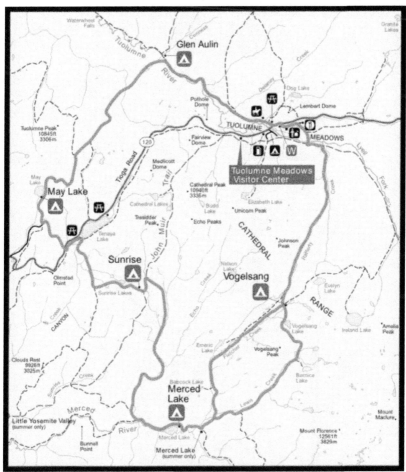

Map of the High Sierra Camp Trails in Yosemite
National Park [Created By James C Heaphy IV]

MAP 6: Yosemite Trail Plan for backpacking

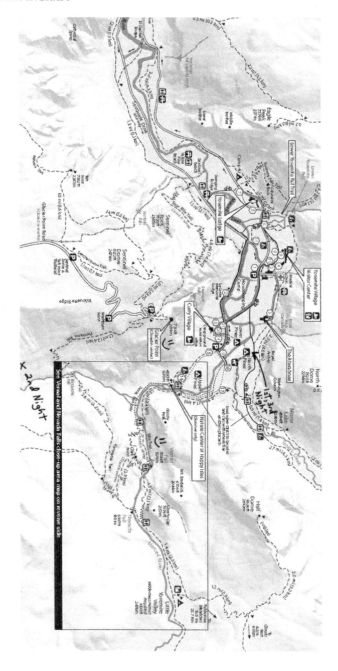

RESOURCEFUL WEBSITES TO VISITING YOSEMITE NATIONAL PARK

There are many resourceful websites to visiting Yosemite National Park. Here are a few of the best:

YOSEMITE NATIONAL PARK WEBSITE

The official website of Yosemite National Park serves as an excellent planning resource for your visit. It offers a wealth of information encompassing park rules, hiking trails, camping areas, and more. Additionally, you can access up-to-date details on weather conditions, road closures, and essential information. The website covers a range of resources, including park information, trip planning, hiking details, camping specifics, weather updates, road conditions, and additional topics such as photography, fishing, and wildlife observation. Utilizing the official Yosemite National Park website, you can efficiently plan a safe and enjoyable trip to this magnificent park.

The official website of Yosemite National Park is https://www.nps.gov/yose/index.htm.

It is managed by the National Park Service, an agency of the United States Department of the Interior..

YOSEMITE CONSERVANCY WEBSITE

Yosemite Conservancy is an organization that operates as a non-profit with the primary aim of safeguarding the natural resources of Yosemite National Park and offering visitors with valuable and rewarding experiences within the park.Their website has a wealth of information on the park's history, geology, and wildlife.
Their official website is https://yosemite.org/

YOSEMITE HIKING WEBSITE

This website is a great resource for hikers planning a trip to Yosemite National Park. It has detailed information on all of the park's trails, including difficulty ratings, elevation profiles, and photos.

Their official website is **https://www.yosemitehikes.com/**

YOSEMITE WEATHER WEBSITE

This website is a great resource for checking the weather forecast for Yosemite National Park. It also has information on the park's climate and weather patterns.

The official website is **https://yosemiteforecast.com/**

<u>CONCLUSION</u>

As we reach the conclusion of this guide to Yosemite National Park, we hope you are filled with excitement and anticipation for your upcoming adventure in this majestic natural wonderland. Yosemite's awe-inspiring landscapes, rich biodiversity, and abundant outdoor activities make it a dream destination for nature lovers, adventure enthusiasts, and those seeking a break from the hustle and bustle of everyday life.

In the various sections of this manual, we have examined the past and importance of Yosemite, delved into its awe-inspiring natural marvels, and offered valuable advice on accommodations, dining, and capturing its picturesque allure with a camera. We have also provided recommendations for staying safe, highlighted activities suitable for families, and uncovered secret treasures eagerly awaiting exploration. Equipped with this information, you are prepared to begin a remarkable adventure that will undoubtedly leave an indelible mark on your emotions and spirit.

As you venture into Yosemite National Park, remember to tread lightly and leave no trace. Respect the natural environment, wildlife, and cultural heritage that make this place so extraordinary. Take the time to immerse yourself in the serenity of nature, whether it's hiking along trails, gazing at waterfalls, or simply sitting in quiet contemplation surrounded by towering granite cliffs.

Yosemite's seasons offer distinct experiences, from the vibrant blooms of spring to the snowy wonderland of winter. Each visit to the park holds new discoveries and opportunities for exploration. The memories you create here, whether it's watching a breathtaking sunset, spotting elusive wildlife, or sharing laughter around a campfire, will stay with you forever.

Yosemite National Park surpasses mere tourism—it serves as a refuge beckoning you to rediscover the wonders of the natural realm and seek solace in its magnificence. It stands as a reminder of the intricate equilibrium between human life and the delicate ecosystems we are privileged to witness. Allow the essence of Yosemite to awaken your curiosity and cultivate a profound gratitude for the extraordinary beauty that envelops us.

May your journey through Yosemite National Park be filled with awe-inspiring moments, thrilling adventures, and a deep sense of connection with nature. Take the time to breathe in the fresh mountain air, listen to the soothing sounds of nature, and let the magnificence of Yosemite leave an indelible mark on your soul.

Safe travels, fellow adventurers, and may your exploration of Yosemite be nothing short of extraordinary.

Printed in Great·Britain
by Amazon

40169221R00079